AF554723

8° V
13

NOTE CIRCULAIRE.

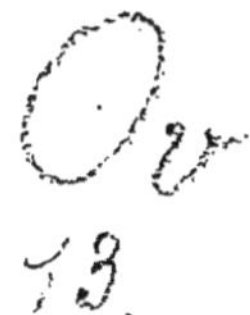

NOTE CIRCULAIRE,

ADDRESSÉE PAR LE

COMTE DE FUNCHAL,

Ambassadeur Extraordinaire, et Plenipotentiaire,

DE S. A. R.

Le Prince Regent de Portugal,

A LEURS EXCELLENCES

MESSIEURS LES AMBASSADEURS, ENVOYES, ET MINISTRES PLENIPOTENTIAIRES,

ACCREDITÉS A LA

COUR DE LONDRES.

BIBLIOTHÈQUE ROYALE I

A LONDRES:

IMPRIMÉ POUR J. BOOKER, NEW BOND STREET,

PAR J. F. DOVE, ST. JOHN'S SQUARE.

1815.

CIRCULAIRE.

Londres, 24 *Mai*, 1815.

LE Comte de Funchal, Ambassadeur Extraordinaire et Plenipotentiaire de S. A. R. le Prince Regent de Portugal a l'honneur d'adresser à Son Excellence Monsieur

l'Exposé, de la Conduite qu' il a tenu à l'occasion d'un Libelle scandaleux publié contre lui en cette Capitale, des motifs qui l'ont determiné, et du premier resultat de ses demarches.

Monsieur est prié d'observer, que le Soliciteur-General de la Couronne Sir S. Shepheard après avoir motivé, dans son Avis ci-joint, et d'une maniere energique, l'obligation morale, dans laquelle Le

Soussigné se trouvait, de poursuivre l'Editeur, a egalement dissipé la seule inquietude qui pouvait retarder sa decision, par l'assurance que l'Intervention du Gouvernement ne devait pas même etre demandée, et que les faits allegués pouvant etre prouvés, sans la presence du Soussigné devant les Cours de Justice, l'Immunité de l'Ambassadeur ne serait, ni enfreinte, ni compromise.

Le Comte de Funchal profite de cette occasion pour reiterer à Son Excellence, Monsieur

l'assurance de Sa Haute Consideration.

Le Comte de Funchal.

A son Excellence Monsieur.

EXPOSÉ.

SIR,

I NOW beg to lay before your Excellency, a statement of the proceedings, in regard to the Libel upon your Excellency, and the Administrators of the affairs of His Royal Highness the Prince Regent of Portugal, published by Mr. Da Costa, in the February Number of the Correio Braziliense. In addition to the translation of the Libel furnished me by your Excellency, I obtained an accurate notarial one, and submitted to the consideration of Sir Samuel Shepheard, His Majesty's Solicitor General. I have the honour to inclose his opinion on the Case, (No. 1.) but this opinion will in some degree be more elucidated, by its being understood, that the Solicitor General's sentiments were required, on different points, namely, 1st. Whether the Administrators alone should adopt legal proceedings, or conjointly with your Excellency; and 2dly. Whether measures which either they, or your Excellency might be recommended to take, should be in the nature of a Civil Action for damages, or by Indictment for the offence. The Solicitor General's opinion your Excellency will find applies to every view of the Case.

In a subsequent conference which I had with the Solicitor General, by the desire of your Excellency, I submitted the following queries for his consideration:—1st. Whether this was not a Case in which the British Government would direct an ex officio Prosecution: 2dly. Whether in the event of your Excellency directing a Prosecution, in conformity to the opinion referred to, it would be a waiver of, or in any manner effect the privileges you possess, and which you considered you ought rigidly to maintain as a Foreign Minister. To the first question, Mr. Solicitor General was of opinion, the intervention of our Government was by no means necessary; and that, in his judgment, had he or his Colleague, His Majesty's Attorney General, been consulted by Government, on such a question, their advice would have been, that although it was a very proper case for your Excellency to prosecute, as the Libel contained a wanton and malicious attack upon your moral integrity, yet that they should not have deemed it prudent, or adviseable, to make it the subject of a Government Prosecution. Upon the latter question, nothing could be more decisive than the opinion of the Solicitor General; as he was quite clear, that your Privileges could in no respect be affected by your appearing either in the character of a Prosecutor, or a Witness in a Court of Justice, although it was entirely unnecessary for you to appear in Court on the occasion, as the Case admitted of other Proofs and Evidence to establish it, than what your Excellency might be able personally to afford. Since the conference I have laid before Mr. Solicitor General the Letter intended to be addressed by your Excellency to Lord Castlereagh; in which you state to his Lordship, the verbal opinion of the Solicitor General as I have detailed it, and which I reported to your Excellency immediately after my consultation. I now have also the honour of inclosing (No. 2.) the Solicitor General's second opinion, and which reduces the subject-matter of the conference alluded to into writing.

In consequence of these opinions, I presented, by the desire of your Excellency, a Bill of Indictment to the Grand Jury at Westminster, but which, from some technical cause (for I think I am at liberty to say it was not upon the merits of the case) was not found. By the advice, however, of the Solicitor General, I presented it to the Grand Jury at Clerkenwell, where it was immediately found a true Bill; and I have since removed it by certiorari into the Court of King's Bench, in which it will, in due course, come on for trial.

Previous to the trial, your Excellency may have an opportunity of meeting at a consultation the Attorney and Solicitor General, for the purpose of taking their further advice how to regulate yourself on this occasion.

I have the honour to remain,

Your Excellency's obedient Servant,

DANIEL ROWLAND.

Gray's Inn Place,
May 19th, 1815.

His Excellency the Count of Funchal,
&c. &c. &c.

Sir,

I beg to inform your Excellency, that nothing more can be done, in respect to the prosecution, until the Defendant has pleaded, and that it would be very informal, and indeed useless and irregular, to have any consultation until the plea comes in.

I remain,

Your Excellency's obedient Servant,

DAN. ROWLAND.

Gray's Inn Place,
20th May, 1815.

OPINION.—No. I.

" I HAVE perused the translation of the li-
" bellous Publication; it is so unintelligibly
" written, with respect to the Administrators,
" that I feel great difficulty in pointing out
" how it can be *stated upon a record*, either in
" a Declaration, or an Indictment, as a libel
" *upon them*. The term '*loaded dice*,' is I
" think clearly meant to be applied to the Ad-
" ministrators, and the natural meaning of
" those words, is not only that they are in-
" struments in the hands of the Ambassador,
" but that they are corrupt instruments; and
" if that *be found* to be the meaning by a Jury,
" it is then a *libel upon them*. Of the two
" modes of proceeding, I rather *advise* an *In-
" dictment*; because it is very *equivocal, to
" which* of the Administrators the Author
" applies the term loaded dice; whether to

" those who served gratuitously for a year, or " to those since appointed, or both ; and in *an* " *Indictment* it might be laid *both ways* ; " besides which, any actions must be separate, " at the suit of each Individual Administrator ; " which would multiply the proceedings.

" Though I have said, an Indictment is the " better course to pursue, yet I think there " will be difficulty, in giving an intelligible " *meaning to the Libel, as applicable* to the " *Administrators*, so as to support an Indict- " ment ; with *respect to his Excellency*, the Por- " tuguese Ambassador, it is a *direct* and *pal-* " *pable* libel on *his moral integrity*, if the " Paper in question contained only strictures " on the Political measures, or conduct of his " Excellency : reflections upon the wisdom of " his conduct, so written as to be libellous, " had perhaps, *generally speaking*, be better past " by ; but the *charge in this publication* is " upon his *moral integrity*, *containing an im-* " *putation of bribery*, *fraud*, and *corruption*. " Upon him, therefore, there is no doubt it is a " Libel ; and unless his Excellency thinks it a

"Publication of too small circulation to be "worth noticing, or entirely beneath his dig- "nity, *it occurs to me that an Indictment,* "*charging the Publication as a libel upon him,* "*and also* as a *libel on the Administrators,* "*would be the proper mode of proceeding;* and "best operate as a check on the libeller in "future.

"I think, also, if the *Administrators only* pro- "secute, it may be observed, that it is *singular* "they should prosecute on an *equivocal charge,* "when the *Ambassador abstains* on a *direct* "one.

"The evidence of the proof sheets being sent "for Publication, corrected in the hand writing "of Da Costa, will be sufficient evidence on "which to convict him of causing the Publica- "tion, but it will be adviseable also to prove "Da Costa to be the Proprietor of the Publi- "cation if possible."

S. SHEPHEARD.

March 17th, 1815.

CASE.---No. II.

SEE the Case left herewith, with the opinion of Mr. Solicitor General thereon :—

After this opinion was taken, a conference was had with Mr. Solicitor General; the result of which was stated in a letter by Mr. Rowland to his Excellency the Count of Funchal, and was also incorporated in a letter intended to be written by the Count of Funchal to Lord Castlereagh.

The letter intended to be addressed by the Count of Funchal to Lord Castlereagh was as follows:

MY LORD,

" I HAVE the honour to inform your Lord-
" ship, that a person of the name of Da Costa,
" who is the author and editor of a periodical

" Portuguese Journal, has, in a recent number, " published a most wanton and flagitious libel " on my moral character; imputing to me " bribery and corruption, and reflecting on my " moral integrity.

" The libel also extends to similar imputa- " tions on the directors of the affairs of His " Royal Highness the Prince Regent of Por- " tugal. This man has, for some years past, " been pursuing a similar line of conduct; but " as his libels have been, for the greater part, " confined to mere personal attacks, and to " animadversions on my politics, I have not " deemed it worth my attention, to direct him " to be prosecuted, although his remarks have " been scurrilous and scandalous in the ex- " treme.

" The paper in question has been laid before " His Britannic Majesty's Solicitor General, " who conceives that I ought to vindicate my " character from the foul aspersions thrown on " it by this libel; and I have accordingly " directed, under that advice, an Indictment " to be exhibited against this delinquent.

" For the information of your Lordship, and " also as a justification for my proceeding, I " should also add, that I understand it distinct- " ly to be the opinion of the Solicitor General, " that the intervention of the Government is not " requisite on this occasion, nor is any appli- " cation from me necessary before I commence " the necessary proceedings. Had I applied to " Government to direct a prosecution in this " case, the Solicitor General is of opinion, both " he and the Attorney General would have ad- " vised that it was not a Case for the inter- " ference of Government, but that the redress " should be personally sought for by me. I " have the same authority for stating to your " Lordship, that this will not amount to any " breach of privilege on my part, and that, " notwithstanding this prosecution, my privi- " lege remains unwaved, even if I were person- " ally to appear in Court, but which appear- " ance is entirely unnecessary."

Although His Excellency is satisfied with the advice given at the conference with Mr. Solicitor General, yet, as he wishes to be minutely accurate in his proceedings on this occasion, both as it respects his own Government and the British Government, and also to act to the satisfaction of the Representatives of the other Governments of Europe, it becomes desirable, that the opinion of Mr. Solicitor General, given at the consultation, should be recorded in writing. One object, therefore, of this Case is, that Mr. Solicitor General should sanction, by his written opinion, the sentiments which are attributed to him in the Letter before set forth, so far as his opinion appears to be quoted, particularly in respect to the two most material points, namely, that the Case of the Libel in question did not appear to be one in which Mr. Solicitor General, or his coadjutor, the Attorney General, would recommend the British Government to direct an *ex officio* prosecution, and that the redress should be sought for by his Excellency personally; and secondly, that His Excellency did not wave or prejudice any privilege that belonged to him in his diplomatic character, by directing a Prosecution for the Libel in question.

Moreover, that such privilege would not be affected by his personal appearance in Court as a witness, though such appearance was not necessary, as the facts admitted of proof without it.

The Bill was presented to the Grand Jury of Middlesex, in the Court of King's Bench, but was lost, for reasons, not as it is believed founded upon the merits of the Case; and, in consequence of that proceeding, His Excellency had a personal conference with Mr. Solicitor General, who advised the presenting of it again to the Grand Jury at Clerkenwell. This was accordingly done, and that Grand Jury accordingly found a true Bill against Mr. Da Costa, for the Libel, and the Indictment has since been removed by the Prosecutor to the Court of King's Bench.

Mr. Solicitor General will be pleased, in writing on this Case, to notice the fact, that on the 8th of May, after the first Bill was lost, he advised the presenting of it again to the Grand Jury at Clerkenwell.

Mr. Solicitor General's Opinion.

" In stating my opinion, that this would be
" a fit subject for Prosecution by Indictment
" by His Excellency the Portuguese Am-
" bassador, it is to be recollected, that I was
" giving it as my opinion as a private Advo-
" cate to a private client; for, if the question
" had been put to me, as one of the advisers
" of the Crown, I should not have given an
" opinion without the sanction and concur-
" rence of the Attorney General. If the ques-
" tion put to me in the Case had been,
" Whether an Information should be filed ex
" officio? I should have declined answering
" that question, for any person not consulting
" me on the part of His Majesty's Govern-
" ment; because, I never give advice to pri-
" vate individuals, however high their rank or
" station, in matters which may afterwards
" come before me, as a Law Officer of the
" Crown; nor to any public functionary in such
" matters, except such questions are put

" through the medium of some of the Offi- " cers of his Majesty's Government. It is " very possible, that in consultation, I sta- " ted, that I thought this was *not a Case* in " which the extraordinary power of His Majes- " ty's Attorney General would be thought " necessary to be exercised; but I beg to be " understood, as not giving that as an opinion " as Solicitor General, for the reasons I have " before given; *though I still think so.*—The " only questions put to me on this part of the " subject by the Case was, *whether an Indict-* " *ment, or an Action at the suit of the Admi-* " *nistrators, were the preferable mode of pro-* " *ceeding?* and I beg to refer to the opinion " on that Case for the answer. *With respect* " to the *present Prosecution affecting* any of " the *privileges* that the Portuguese Ambassa- " dor is entitled to, I am of opinion, the re- " sorting to the protection of the Law, either " by prosecuting a Civil Action, or Indictment, " *can never infringe any of his privileges.* The " preferring the Indictment to the Grand Jury " at the Sessions House, after the Bill had "been thrown out by the Grand Jury at "Westminster, was by my advice, because "I thought the Grand Jury had judged "erroneously, in returning the Bill not "found. The Grand Jury having found the "Bill, the Indictment for the Libel must be "tried by another Jury, and they must de- "cide upon its merits, in the same manner as "Juries by the constitution of this Country, "have power to do, on all Prosecutions for "Libels, whether instituted by way of Indict- "ment, information granted by the King's "Bench, or information filed ex officio; for "the power, and mode, of ultimately deciding "upon the guilt or innocence of the party "accused, is the same in all: nor can there "be any distinction of persons in this re- "spect by the English Law.—It certainly "was not necessary that His Excellency the "Portuguese Ambassador should make any "application to His Majesty's Government, "before he instituted this Prosecution, *nor do* "*I think* he *can be considered* as having com-

"promised any of his rights by not doing so:
'having reason to complain of a libellous publication, he is perfectly justified, in every point of view, in resorting to the ordinary process of the Law for redress.

BIBLIOTHÈQUE ROYALE

T. S. SHEPHEARD.

May 18, 1815.

Printed by J. F. Dove, St. John's Square.

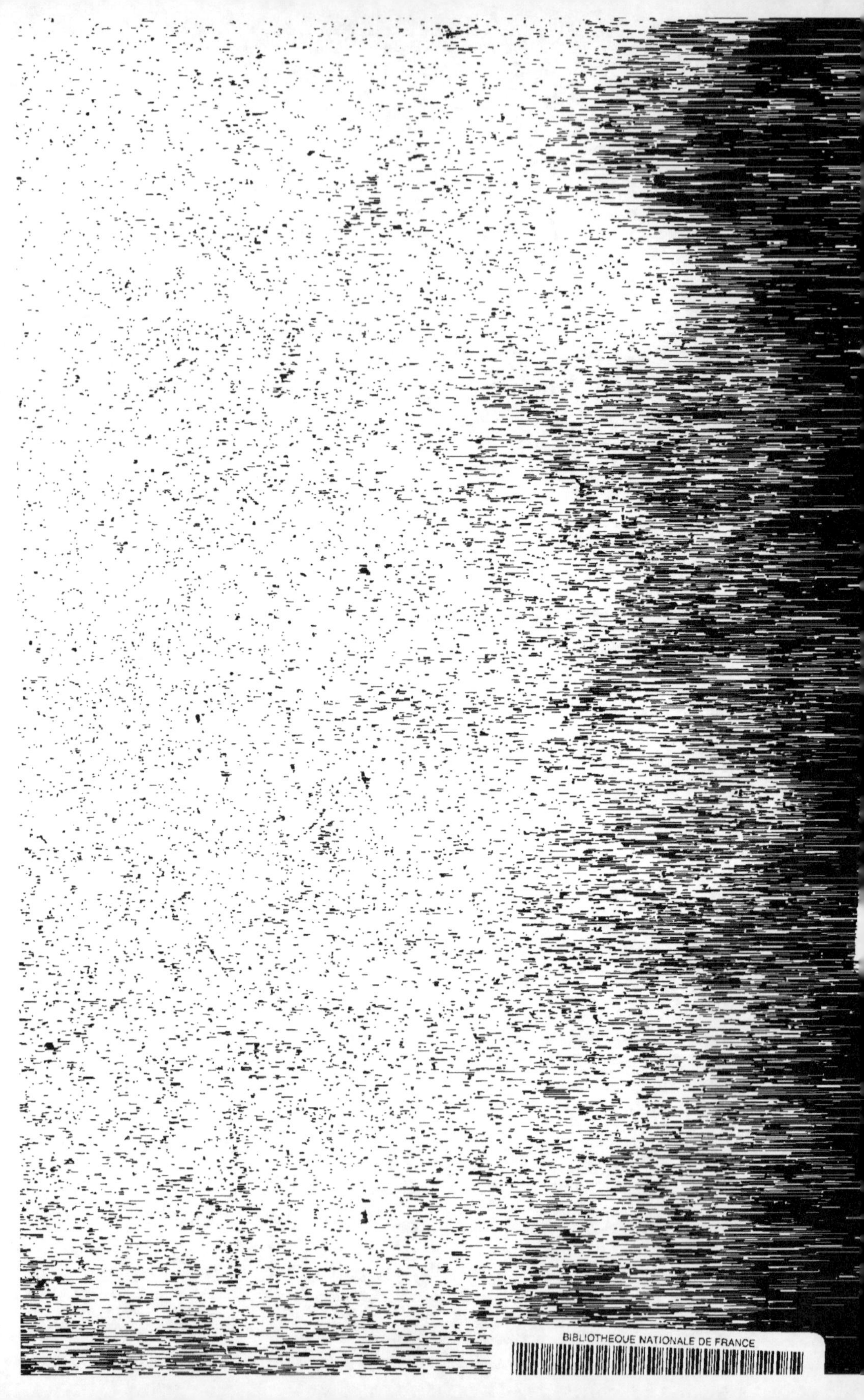
BIBLIOTHEQUE NATIONALE DE FRANCE

www.ingramcontent.com/pod-product-compliance
Lightning Source LLC
LaVergne TN
LVHW010308230826
846091LV00007BB/2775

* 9 7 8 2 0 1 3 3 4 0 1 1 3 *